Florida

A Journey Through its Colorful Past

TEXT AND PHOTOGRAPHY BY
Patty DiRienzo

WESTCLIFFE PUBLISHERS
www.bigearthpublishing.com

Published by Westcliffe Publishers, Inc.
a Big Earth Publishing company
3005 Center Green Drive, Suite 220
Boulder, Colorado 80301

ISBN: 978-1-56579-622-5

Cover and text design: Rebecca Finkel
Text and photography: © Patty DiRienzo, 2008.
All rights reserved.
Printed in China through Imago

For more information about other fine books and calendars
from Westcliffe Publishers, a Big Earth Publishing company,
please contact your local bookstore, call us at 1-800-258-5830,
or visit us on the Web at bigearthpublishing.com.

Library of Congress Cataloging-in-Publication Data: On file.

For Pete and Mary,

who taught me the value of

life's simple pleasures.

Introduction

"The City of Green Benches" and old folks. St. Petersburg sure had a hard time shaking that reputation. But by the end of the 20th century, St. Pete's demographic was much younger, and the green benches that once lined downtown streets had long since disappeared. What didn't change about this revitalized city was something untouchable—its sense of place.

My husband and I lived in St. Pete's Old Northeast, the oldest neighborhood in the city, known for its brick streets and live oaks. Just steps from downtown, we often strolled our young daughter along city sidewalks, passing such historic treasures as the lavishly designed Snell Arcade and the weathered St. Petersburg Lawn Bowling Club. We felt lucky to live in a city where reminders of its colorful past were all around us.

But as gratifying as it was to have these historic buildings as part of our everyday lives, their future sparked numerous debates among residents and city officials. Some landmarks lost their battle to the pressures of progress. We watched the vintage Soreno Hotel come crashing down to accommodate plans for new downtown development. Still, other landmarks came out on the winning side with beautifully restored facades and a new generation of fans. After a $93 million restoration, the once-abandoned 1925 Vinoy Park Hotel is once again the centerpiece of a booming downtown.

This same kind of debate between saving the old or bulldozing a path for the new is being waged in dozens of Florida communities. A prime example is American Beach, Florida's first African-American beach community. Threatened by the encroachment of mega-resorts on both sides, this shrinking town fought back. The founder's great granddaughter, MaVynee Betsch, rallied neighbors, government officials, and even the resorts in an effort to preserve her town's history. Recently listed on the National Register of Historic Places, American Beach is hoping for a brighter future.

In my eyes, Florida is slowly losing its unique heritage, leaving behind the very people and places that make it such a fascinating destination. Dwindling numbers of citrus groves, ranches, offbeat attractions, and cigar factories still dot Florida's landscape. As a photojournalist, creatively documenting these unassuming landmarks and the people who know them best is my way of preserving Old Florida. To truly capture the spirit of these aging landmarks, I used a hand-crafted photo process —Polaroid image transfer. It allowed me to give a modern day photograph a vintage feel.

While traveling Florida's back roads and interstates, my goal was to feature a variety of hometown landmarks, from the Panhandle to the Keys. Some are modest and unobtrusive, like the ramshackle fish camp along the Chassahowitzka River. Others beg for attention, like the flashing neon Pensacola Beach welcome sign. Some locations are listed in the National Register of Historic Places. Others hold legendary status within their own community. No matter what their historical designation, all represent the heart and soul of Florida.

By far, the highlight of my travels was getting to know the 'old timers' who shared their insight about Florida, then and now. It was inspiring to hear their tales of hardship and comradery, good times and simple pleasures. A lighthouse keeper's daughter said it best. "We had such freedom. We fished, we shelled, we climbed trees. We wore no shoes to school . . . . I didn't realize that everyone's childhood was not like mine."

I was left with a new respect for those who came before us and a deep appreciation for their Old Florida lifestyle. Most importantly, their heartfelt remembrances brought life to otherwise hushed buildings and gathering places.

Sadly, some Floridians who shared their time and memories have passed on. I was particularly touched by the passing of Key's fishing guide Cecil Keith. A respected fisherman and guide for over 50 years, his ashes were scattered on the shallow waters of the backcountry where he spent the best days of his life. A parade of boats and fellow fishermen joined in to say good-bye to a Key's legend.

As you take this journey down the back roads and city streets of Old Florida, I hope the spirit of these pioneers and their cherished landmarks brings you closer to understanding the secrets of Florida's past and the challenges of her future.

Let's celebrate the "City of Green Benches"—and all the landmarks that give every corner of Florida its unique sense of place.

Pensacola

Tallahassee

10

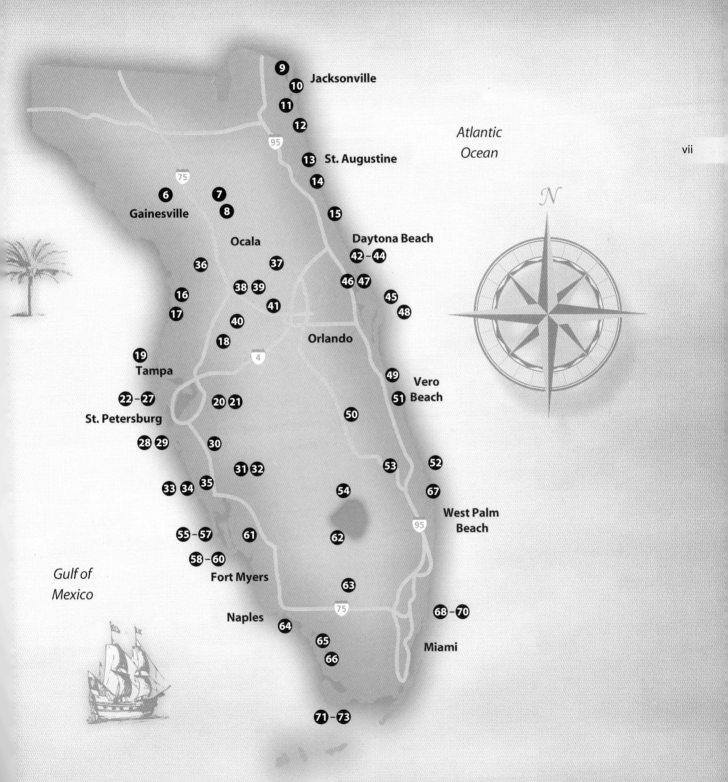

Pensacola Beach Welcome Sign

1955–Present • Pensacola Beach

"You couldn't miss it, it got your attention. . . . I first noticed the sign when it was downtown. The purpose of putting it there was to remind people, 'You have a beautiful beach. Use it!' . . . It seemed like such a long drive out to the beach back then. It encouraged people to come over to the beach and enjoy it and make it profitable. . . . Later, the sign was moved out near the new bridge to the beach. As a child, I would see it and think, 'Okay, we're almost there!' . . . I always loved the beach. My mother has lots of pictures of me in diapers, as brown as I could be, sitting on that white sand."

—Sandy Johnston, native of Pensacola and executive director
of the Pensacola Beach Chamber of Commerce

High atop a building in downtown Pensacola, a vibrant neon sign flashed the wonders of Pensacola Beach. Enthusiastic beach officials and Lamar Advertising strategically placed the sign miles inland to urge residents and visitors to take a beach break. In the 1950s, in-town activities were plentiful, so venturing out to Pensacola's white sand beaches and its fledgling amusements was a stretch. A decade later, the memorable sailfish sign was moved closer to the shore. Now located on US 98, the sign has welcomed tourists to the blue-green waters and sparkling sands of Pensacola Beach for almost 50 years.

Apalachicola

1831–Present · Apalachicola

"*Living used to be easy. You could always get your meal off the water. . . . I started working down on the water when I was six, breaking heads off shrimp. For fun, I came down here every day and swam all the way across the river. . . . When I was older, during fishing season, I shucked oysters and picked crab. . . . Everybody was just trying to make a living—women, men, and children . . . . This place was wide-open back then. There were bars—but moonshine was more convenient. . . . It was a tight-knit community. This town wasn't integrated back then, but everybody got along.*"

—Sebron James, native of Apalachicola

Where the fresh-water Apalachicola River meets the salty bay, Mother Nature serves up a shellfish feast. The cotton industry was the first to take hold in pre–Civil War Apalachicola. Plantations sent bales of cotton downriver to the port of Apalachicola, where they shipped out to mills across the ocean. Sponges and lumber also played major roles in the area's economy, but it was the seafood industry in the late 1800s that became Apalachicola's most memorable resource. The bay's warm, shallow waters produced an abundance of flavorful oysters, shrimp, and blue crab. A dedicated workforce of fishermen and processors brought the harvest to the table. Apalachicola oysters still hold the top spot among chefs and consumers worldwide.

Canopy Roads

Tallahassee, Leon County

"Our road was an antebellum cotton route. It's still dirt and we're proud of it. . . . In my daddy's generation, you worked from sunup to sundown. When you walked somewhere was when you felt more carefree . . . everyone walked. It was four miles to school, five miles to church, and another four miles to the baseball field. . . . When the first automobiles appeared on the road, we had our favorite tricks. We caught a black snake, put it in a purse, and laid it on the road. Every automobile picked it up and slammed on the brakes. It was our entertainment! . . . There was excitement when the 'rolling store' came down the road—it was like a one-aisle store that sold anything you couldn't grow on the farm. It had the best cinnamon rolls. . . . There's something special about the beauty and serenity of these roads. They give you a sense of place."

—Lane Green. Since the 1860s, the Green family has made their home on Sunny Hill Road, a canopy road in northern Leon County.

Less than 20 miles from the Georgia border, Florida looks more like the Old South than a beachgoer's paradise. Draped in live oaks and Spanish moss, Tallahassee's designated canopy roads radiate out from town through woods and pastures. These routes, once traveled by both Apalachee Indians and Spanish explorers, started out as little more than footpaths through the wilderness. By the late 1800s, these clay-packed routes served plantation owners transporting cotton and crops to market. Nine of the rudimentary roads, including Miccosukee, Old St. Augustine, and Sunny Hill, eventually became thoroughfares for mule-driven wagons heading to port towns. Today, Leon County continues to value and protect its canopy roads.

Bradley's Country Store

1927–Present • Tallahassee

"My grandmother started making sausage in 1910. We still use her recipe today—if it ain't broke, don't fix it. . . . My dad raised his own hogs. He killed two hogs a week—three if business was good. . . . In the '40s, my father peddled sausage at the state buildings and banks in Tallahassee. When he got too old and Tallahassee got too big, my father said, 'They can come out here and get it!' . . . Saturday was our big day—the lot was full of wagons, buggies, and people on horseback. . . . There were no paved roads into Tallahassee."*

—Frank Bradley, grandson of Mary Bradley,
whose sausage recipe was the inspiration for Bradley's Country Store

What began as a Bradley family recipe in 1910 ended up as a Tallahassee tradition. It didn't take long for word to spread about Grandma Mary's seasoned sausage. She sold her first samples right out of the Bradley Farm kitchen. The popularity of her recipe jumpstarted other Bradley ventures, including a gristmill where local farmers gathered for "corn grindin'." In 1927, the family opened a storefront to market their growing number of products. Four generations later, Bradley's Country Store remains a popular stop on one of Tallahassee's historic canopy roads.

Wakulla Springs Lodge

1937–Present • Wakulla Springs

"There wasn't much going on out here in the old days. . . . *We looked at it as a privilege to work at the lodge. It was the cream of the crop. . . . In the early days it was a retreat, a place for relaxation. . . . Dignitaries, congressmen, and judges came out here from Tallahassee. . . . The owner, Edward Ball, was a preserver of wildlife—it was like a refuge. . . . My father did boat tours and was groundskeeper. He laid the pavers in the walk by hand. You might see his name on them: 'Woodrow'. . . . In the '40s, underwater scenes for some Tarzan movies were filmed right here in the deep spring. The wildlife scenes were shot back there in the jungle. . . .* Creature from the Black Lagoon *was also filmed here."*

—Donald Gavin, native of Wakulla County and veteran boat tour guide

In the early twentieth-century, naturalists soaked up the untamed beauty of Wakulla Springs just south of Tallahassee. That same raw beauty prompted powerful businessman Edward Ball to buy up the springs and 4,000 acres surrounding it. Wildlife thrives in and around this deep spring, where water gushes at 400,000 gallons per minute. In 1937, Ball put his money to work building a Mediterranean-style retreat overlooking the spring. With its marble floors, beamed ceilings, and imported ceramic tile, Wakulla Springs Lodge offers guests a touch of elegance in the wilderness. Ball fenced off the spring to discourage boaters, a controversial move that has helped preserve the spring's fragile ecosystem.

Dudley Farm

1850s–1940s · Newberry

"The corn we grow on the farm is the same seed that Miss Myrtle Dudley handed down to us. She was the last born of 12 children. . . . On the farm, everybody had chores. The kids milked cows and churned butter. . . . They had to keep the yard around the house 'swept' as a safeguard against forest fires. The older kids took care of the younger ones, and they washed, ironed, and cooked. . . . When asked, Myrtle Dudley would say, 'It was just the way of life. We didn't realize it was hard.' . . . The Dudleys were very self-sufficient . . . they even built the road to Gainesville. Cattle drives, mule carts—everybody came down that road. And the Dudleys put their general store on it to take advantage of the traffic. They were important to the whole community."

—Terry Stidham, sixth-generation Floridian and park ranger
at Dudley Farm Historic State Park

At sunup, the 14-member Dudley clan came together like a well-oiled machine. Not only did their 640-acre farm outside of Gainesville produce enough food for their large family, it supplied the needs of families for miles around beginning in 1880. Using lumber from their land, the Dudleys built a sprawling homestead that included a general store and post office. Their crops changed through the years according to demand, but sweet potatoes, corn, and sugar cane were staples. When farming became mechanized in the 1920s, the Dudleys traded two mules and some cash for their first tractor. Three generations of Dudleys lived off the land, raising livestock, cultivating crops, and selling their goods. Today, Dudley Farm continues its legacy as the Dudley Farm Historic State Park, where visitors can experience early Florida farm life.

Prairie Creek at Newnan's Lake

Gainesville

"Grandpa was a bass master, one hell of a bass angler. He was a big tournament fisherman, and Newnan's Lake was one of the largest bigmouth bass lakes anywhere. . . . I caught my first bass here with him . . . we used heavy boats called 'Stump-nockers.' They're good for hitting up against cypress knees, and they last forever. . . . The lake was so big, it created its own weather. If the wind came up, you ended up against the stumps on the side of the lake. . . . Grandpa used to tell a story about the water moccasins hanging in the trees around the lake—a snake would fall into a fisherman's boat and some moron would panic and shoot the snake. Of course, then the boat would sink, and the gators would get him!"*

—Monica Carter, owns and operates Kate's Fish Camp
along with her husband, Michael

In 2000, North America's largest grouping of ancient canoes surfaced from under a blanket of mud in drought-stricken Newnan's lake, located just east of Gainesville. Many of the 86 canoes dated between 3,000 and 5,000 years old. Canoes still float the waters today, carrying modern-day anglers who cast their lines for largemouth bass and enjoy the plentiful wildlife that inhabit the lake's cypress-lined shores. In the 1960s, Kate's Fish Camp took up residence on Prairie Creek, one of the lake's natural waterways. They serve up bait, beer, and boats to eager fishermen heading out for a day on the water.

Wood & Swink General Store
and Post Office

1882–Present • Evinston

"*This is Evinston. Any business or gossip that comes up is done right here—we get to see everyone in town at least once a week. . . . When my father took over the store and post office in 1933, he kept the mail in cigar boxes. . . . When he heard the whistle blow, dad would hang the mail sack from a 'crane' across the road at the train depot. A steam locomotive came by, stuck out a bar, and pulled it in. . . . We still have shotgun pellets in the ceiling from the time someone received a gun in the mail and started fooling around with it. . . . Our store had a little bit of everything—clothing, groceries, cattle and mule feed. In daddy's time, he butchered pigs in the winter and sold whole hogs in here. We had a neighbor who ate every part of the pig. Mom used to say, 'The only thing wasted was the squeal!'*"

—Fred Wood Jr. third generation of the Wood Family
to operate the Wood & Swink General Store and Post Office

In 1906, H.D. Wood purchased the Post Office in rural Evinston, christening it the Wood & Swink and expanding it to include a general store. For nearly a century, the Wood family has served up mail, groceries, and a friendly ear, operating as the hub of activity in this close-knit farming community set among the lakes of north-central Florida. Built from heart of pine in the late 1800s, this unassuming building holds the record for the oldest post office in the state.

Palace Saloon

1903–Present · Fernandina Beach

"Fernandina was strictly a fishing and shipping town in 1878. There were 22 bars, and they all catered to sailors. . . . The Palace Saloon was set out to be a cut above the rest. It was built to cater to the ships' officers. . . . Its bar was made of mahogany and English oak. . . . When I owned the bar, it was a real mixing pot. You might see a shrimper sitting next to someone from a resort hotel. . . . Somebody was always interested in what you had to say. . . . It was the old neighborhood bar, but it wasn't cliquish or clannish. Even the workers who came off ships from all over the world felt comfortable here."
—Aubrey Williams, Palace Saloon proprietor, 1970-80

In a town where the shipping industry and its rabble-rousing sailors were king, the Palace Saloon reigned supreme. Out of about 20 bars in town, the Palace Saloon was Fernandina's only first-class watering hole. In 1903, owner Louis Hirth spared no expense outfitting the saloon with a mahogany bar, embossed tin ceilings, mosaic floors, and hand-painted murals. Not only did the saloon serve high-ranking sailors, it attracted high-powered families like the DuPonts, the Carnegies, and the Vanderbilts. Even during the prohibition years, the Palace Saloon managed to earn its keep and was later christened "Florida's oldest bar." In business for over a century, The Palace Saloon still lives up to its long-standing reputation for excellence.

American Beach

1935–Present · American Beach, Amelia Island

"The insurance company might have bought the land, but American Beach was intended for all blacks. There was nowhere else for us to go. . . . It was a bustling place, like one big party. 'Yellow hounds'—school buses—would bring in people from all over to spend a week or a weekend at the beach. . . . You could come and find everything you needed. We had restaurants, airplane rides, a jukebox, and dancing. . . . When I sit on my front porch and look out at the ocean, I feel like I'm part of this universe. All my cares and problems seem to disappear."*

—Ernestine Smith, granddaughter of Louis Dargan Ervin, vice president of Afro-American Life Insurance Company. He built his family home, "Ervin's Rest," in 1938 on the shores of American Beach.

It's no surprise that Florida's reputation as a tropical paradise brought in visitors from across the states. But rules of segregation kept African-Americans at arm's length from Florida's palm-lined shores. That is, until the state's first African-American millionaire, A.L. Lewis, bought up a 200-acre parcel of Amelia Island in 1935. From this oceanfront property, he created American Beach, a retreat for employees of his Jacksonville-based Afro-American Insurance Company. It was a bit out of the way, but American Beach offered his workers their own beachfront getaway, complete with cottages for sale. Word spread quickly, prompting African-Americans from across the country to recharge at the restaurants, night clubs, and amusements found there. Cab Calloway, Ray Charles, and Hank Aaron were among the beach's many famous guests.

Singleton's Seafood Shack

1967–Present • Mayport

"My husband was born in a houseboat on the Saint John's River. He was on the water all his life. He was so salty! . . . Ray started out with a party boat, taking passengers deep sea fishing. I went fishing on his boat, got hooked, and he reeled me in! . . . We had a fish market with only five tables. People came in, picked out a fish, and we'd cook it for them. . . . Every year Ray added on to the restaurant, using whatever he had on hand. Every window was different. . . . He always said, 'If you give a quality product at a good price, there are three things people won't do without: fishing, drinking, and eating!' . . . When he had to stop fishing, Ray built [model] boats—about 200 of them. He was good with his hands—he used no plans or measurements."

—Ann Singleton, wife of Ray Singleton, founder of Singleton's Seafood Shack

Located on the Saint John's River and championed for serving up fresh fish just off the boat, Singleton's grew from a simple fish market into a folksy restaurant. Mayport native and Singleton's founder Ray Singleton had a lifelong romance with the sea, working as charter captain, shrimper, and seafood purveyor. After his fishing days were cut short due to the loss of his leg, Captain Ray rebounded with another talent: model boat building. A natural craftsman, he replicated boats from his childhood memories, proudly displaying them at Singleton's. Diners gathered around Captain Ray to marvel at his handiwork and hear his fish tales as he performed his craft.

American Red Cross
Volunteer Lifeguard Station

1912–Present · Jacksonville Beach

"Every lifeguard has a day he'll never forget. . . . It was July, 1964. There were severe run-outs and a lot of swimmers were in trouble. . . . I saw this young boy fall off his raft. As I was bringing him in, he fell off my buoy. I dove down to get him. When I got him ashore, I was shaking him, asking if he was all right. But he just stared at me. Later, his mother told me he was deaf. I just wanted to hug him. . . . It was a miracle, and a lot of teamwork, that nobody drowned that day."

—Steve Park, retired member of American Red Cross Volunteer
Lifeguard Station in Jacksonville Beach

The early 1900s marked a turning point in Florida outdoor recreation, particularly in Jacksonville Beach. Hundreds flocked to the oceanfront for sun, sand, and surf. But along with large numbers of beachgoers came a sharp increase in drowning deaths. In 1912, a concerned local doctor and a playground director created an all-volunteer life saving corps—the first group of its kind in the country. Known for its pioneering efforts in ocean rescue and water safety, the corps developed the "torpedo" buoy, a staple of lifesaving for nearly a century. These well-trained volunteers continue to patrol the Jacksonville Beach shoreline seven days a week.

St. Augustine Alligator Farm

1893–Present · St. Augustine

"Some people came to Florida just to see alligators. . . . *I'm just a kid who grew up in Florida and wound up taking care of a thousand alligators! . . . I remember St. Augustine before the tourists—people stopped to get gas, a Coke, and kept heading south. . . . The Alligator Farm was just a roadside zoo . . . it has always been the best place to get up close to alligators. That's why so much film work and reptile research has been done here through the years. . . . When we do a feeding show, the alligators anticipate food and start jumping up out of the water—you can hear them crunching bones . . . it's those great big gators and those great big teeth. People just can't resist them."*

—Bill Puckett, native Floridian and former director of St. Augustine Alligator Farm

Evolving from a kitschy beachside attraction to a respected animal park, St. Augustine Alligator Farm has indulged our fascination with Florida's most famous reptile for more than a century. Fires and storms threatened its early ocean-side existence, and in 1937 new owners W.I. Drysdale and F. Charles Usina established an inland home for St. Augustine Alligator Farm, which featured not only alligators but a variety of wildlife. Widespread publicity about the park during the '40s and '50s prompted researchers to pursue close-up studies of this one-of-a-kind collection of captive gators. Placed on the endangered species list in the late 1960s, alligators made a complete recovery, partially due to the understanding gained from this research. Even today, education and conservation play important roles in the day-to-day business of St. Augustine Alligator Farm.

St. Augustine Lighthouse

1874–Present • St. Augustine

"*Back in 1928,* *there was a hurricane—I was just a young girl. My mother was in the hospital and my father was on watch. I slept in the top of the tower that night under the lens. My dad laid down his overcoat for me to sleep on. I was scared, but lighthouses are supposed to be one of the safest places. You know, they sway a little. Afterwards, we couldn't get to town for three days. . . . My dad had a great big brass key that opened the door to the tower. One keeper went up at sundown and got the light going—he stayed until one o'clock. Then he rang a bell and the next keeper stayed until sunup. . . . One time my dad was painting the lighthouse all the way up to the lightning rod. I thought my mother was going to have a heart attack, watching my father swing around up there!*"

—Rachel Daniels Lightsey, daughter of "Allie" Daniels,
St. Augustine Lighthouse keeper from 1926–32

In the 1500s the Spanish marked the port of St. Augustine's entrance with a guard tower; that same structure became a full-fledged lighthouse in 1824. With this transformation, St. Augustine became the site of Florida's first lighthouse. During the Civil War, Confederate Floridians extinguished the light and smuggled away the lens to hinder Union forces. The sea eventually claimed the original tower, but the black-and-white-spiraled version of St. Augustine Lighthouse still standing today was completed in 1874. Towering 14 stories above Anastasia Island and topped with a lens standing almost 10 feet tall, the St. Augustine Lighthouse is visible to mariners 20 miles out at sea.

Marineland of Florida

1938–Present · Marineland

"I was a school teacher.... There was an ad in the paper for an apprentice [dolphin] trainer, so I started at the bottom. ... For me, the thrill was working outside by the ocean every day with such great animals. I looked at the dolphins as my co-workers—they knew me quite well. ... When Marineland opened, it was the only place of its kind in the world—it made the magazines from here to France. ... One of the owners was Cornelius Vanderbilt Whitney—he produced Gone with the Wind. *... Marineland was built as a photographic studio for movies—he built the big tank to look like the ocean. ... An animal trainer from Ringling Brothers Circus was hired on to see if he could train the first dolphin. ... This has always been an amazing place with amazing people."*

—Bill Epson, Marineland dolphin trainer and operations supervisor for almost 30 years

Peering through portholes of the world's first "oceanarium," curious tourists got eye-to-eye with creatures of the deep. Never before had an aquarium of this magnitude offered a close-up look at the undersea world. That's why 20,000 people flocked to opening day at Marine Studios (later renamed Marineland) on SR A1A in 1938. Its visionary founders also promoted Hollywood moviemaking in this ready-made underwater studio. *Creature From the Black Lagoon,* released in 1954, was filmed in the park's largest tank. To top off its list of accomplishments, Marineland presented Flippy, the first trained dolphin, in the early 1960s. As expected, tourists streamed in to marvel at this spectacle, landing Marineland the title "Florida's most popular theme park."

Chassahowitzka River

Citrus County

"I fell in love with the Chassahowitzka. . . . I was on the river from the time I was about 11—it was untouched. You could walk out your front door and pick up oysters. . . . It was the best duck hunting place in the world. People came from all over. . . . The Strickland boys spent most of their day in a net boat, mullet fishing—they got five cents a piece for them . . . when you were netting mullet, you had to sneak up on them. They'd fight to get back in the spring. . . . The creeks are the purest part of the river. One goes right through the swamp. And when you break out of the woods, it opens up into the most beautiful spring. It's just like the Indians left it."

—Pye Conrad, born in Inverness and raised along the
Chassahowitzka River in Citrus County

From its still-water swamps to its hidden springs, The Chassahowitzka River is an inviting habitat for wildlife and a welcome escape for city folks. Early on, Floridians realized the importance of preserving this pristine waterway for the migratory birds and ducks that wintered on Florida's central west coast. In 1943, over 31,000 acres of river, salt marsh, swamp, and hardwood hammock were set aside, and the Chassahowitzka National Wildlife Refuge was born. Manatees, black bears, wading birds, and a variety of marine life call the refuge home. The Chassahowitzka offers today's Floridians a recreational retreat for fishing, hunting, and boating.

Weeki Wachee Springs

1946–Present · Weeki Wachee

"*When I was in tenth grade,* I went to see the mermaids with my sister—from then on I wanted to be one . . . it was magical. It wasn't like a real job, except in winter. Back then, we had to run out into the cold to get from the dressing room to the spring. . . . I was a certified scuba diver, so it should have been easy for me, but it wasn't. Being a mermaid was nothing like diving. . . . Sometimes manatees, otters, or turtles would come through during our show. One time we couldn't swim because there was an 8-foot alligator in the spring. . . . Mermaids on the Moon *and* Snow White were two of the shows we performed . . . . Still, every time I see that spring and walk in that theatre—it's magical."

—Billie Fuller, Weeki Wachee Springs mermaid from 1968–9

For the mythical mermaid, there may have been no better home on Earth than Weeki Wachee Springs. In 1946, former Navy frogman instructor Newton Perry chose this picturesque site along US 19 to create a one-of-a-kind roadside attraction. He trained beautiful women to perform in chilly waters while breathing through strategically placed air tubes. From a small, windowed theatre built below water level, visitors got an underwater view of Perry's mermaids as they danced among the currents. Weeki Wachee quickly became a must-see attraction in the 1950s. Not even Elvis Presley could resist a peek.

Joy-Lan Drive-In Theatre

1949–Present • Dade City

"A bunch of kids from school would get together, *borrow a convertible—a turquoise and cream Ford Fairlane 500— and go to the drive-in. It was so much fun . . . to me, the screen was so much bigger than a movie theatre, and you could have a conversation with the person sitting next to you. . . . You had to roll up your window just enough to hook on the amplifier, and your food tray went on the other side. . . . The minute we went down to the snack bar, we saw friends—it was the place to be. . . . The second movie I ever saw was at the Joy-Lan—it was* Love Me Tender *with Elvis Presley."*
— Sylvia Young, lifelong resident of Dade City

With the creation of the drive-in theater, Florida's balmy nights proved ideal for outdoor movie-watching. By the mid-1950s, over 150 drive-ins operated statewide. The Floyd Theatre chain led the way, operating both indoor and outdoor movie theaters in central Florida. The Joy-Lan, a one-screen Floyd Theater built in 1949 on well-traveled US 301, was Dade City's favorite weekend entertainment spot. Rural Pasco County residents also made the trip into town for the chance to watch a movie, eat some popcorn, and socialize with friends and neighbors. When Hurricane Donna hit Florida in 1960 with over 100 mph winds, Floyd Theatres lost five drive-in screens.

St. Nicholas III Sponge Diving Boat

1935–Present · Tarpon Springs

"My grandfather and father came over from Greece at the turn of the century. Sponge diving was a father-to-son trade. . . . My family was part of the original group that came over for the sponge industry. . . . A sponge diver can walk anywhere from one to five miles along the bottom, searching for sponges. You almost jump up and down with joy when you accidentally fall on an area that no one has hit for years. . . . It's another world down there. It's quiet and beautiful, but it can be treacherous. . . . Tourism came about here because of the Greek culture and the sponge industry. . . . Tarpon Springs is a jewel—you feel like you're in two countries at the same time."
—George Billiris, third-generation sponge diver

When Florida's sponge industry was just beginning to take off in the early 1900s, the Greeks were already experts in the art of sponge harvesting. So when the Gulf Coast town of Tarpon Springs wanted to increase its presence in the world's sponge trade, it called in the experts. Armed with the latest in sponge fishing technology, Greek immigrants donned their heavy brass helmets and helped popularize sponge diving in America. By the 1930s, Tarpon Springs was a bustling community with a fleet of nearly 200 sponge diving boats and a variety of businesses to support the industry, earning it the title "sponge capital of the world." The Billiris family, foundational to Tarpon Springs' sponge industry, built St. Nicholas III in 1935 for both sponge diving and tourist excursions.

Ybor City

1885–Present • Tampa

"My father arrived from Cuba in 1905 . . . a cigar warehouse owner made an agreement in which my father would get free room and board if he worked for him. He was 15 years old when he entered the factory . . . he started at the bottom and worked his way up to rolling cigars. . . . In the factory, there were lectores *who read to the workers. Some had beautiful voices . . . sometimes they translated the newspaper. In the afternoons, they read novels from Spain. It kept the workers happy and informed. . . . Compared to what they have in today's factories, they had a beautiful way of life. . . . Our fathers took great pride in being called* tabaqueros, *or cigar makers. Tampa was known as the 'fine cigar capital of the world,' with emphasis on the word 'fine.' "*

—Frank Lastra, born and raised in Ybor City

Cubans, Spaniards, and Italians came together to produce the world's best cigars in Tampa's Ybor City. Although Havana and Key West were first to lead the way in cigar production, Ybor City took over the reins in 1886 with the arrival of Spaniard Vincent Martinez Ybor. Moving his labor-troubled Key West factory north to Tampa, he rallied cigar workers by creating a community that catered to their everyday needs and cultural diversity. Housing, shops, and social clubs made up their thriving neighborhoods. In turn, these hard-working artisans produced the finest of cigars. With its warm weather, deep water port, and railroad, Tampa supported almost 150 cigar factories at the height of the industry. Tampa incorporated Ybor City in 1987. Ybor City is still a thriving area of shops, restaurants, and preserved buildings.

J.C. Newman Cigar Company

1895–Present • Ybor City, Tampa

"I was the one who started the factory down here in Tampa. It was like a furnace! It was hot, but I knew being closer to Cuba, the tobacco wouldn't dry out or lose its aroma and taste. . . . My dad wanted to be in the premium cigar business. Outside of Tampa, there was no other place making or selling premium cigars. . . . Cigar factories were built lining up east to west. The north side of the building was always biggest because you needed the north light to differentiate the shades of cigars. . . . When factories were built, so were all the homes around it. Everyone walked to work. . . . There was the Cuban Club, the Spanish Club, and the Italians. . . . The social life on Seventh Avenue was lively."

—Stanford Newman, son of J.C. Newman,
who established J.C. Newman Cigar Company

J.C. Newman advanced from apprentice cigar maker to cigar company owner by age 20. Rolling cigars in his backyard barn, Newman made his first sale to the local grocery in 1895. Two decades later, Newman was rolling hundreds of cigars a day with the help of 700 workers in 3 factories. Although the Newman family called Cleveland home, Newman took a chance at age 78 and made the decision to relocate his business to Tampa, "the cigar capital." Warm, humid weather and easy access to Cuba sealed the deal. Three generations of family followed in their founder's footsteps, making J.C. Newman the oldest family-owned cigar company in the country.

Sunken Gardens

1903–Present • St. Petersburg

"Mr. Turner loved plants and grew some beautiful gardens—he finally started charging people to come in and see them. . . . We lived five blocks away. Every Saturday my brother and I rode our bikes to Sunken Gardens. We would hide them under the bougainvillea and climb the wall. . . . There were lots of birds, flamingos, monkeys, and alligators. But my favorite place was the gift shop. It was full of all kinds of figurines made out of shells, and tacky souvenirs. . . . The best thing was the orange blossom perfume. When I think about Florida, I think of the smell of that perfume."

—Lauren Martinez, lifelong St. Petersburg resident

In 1903, plumber George Turner's love of gardening prompted him to buy a five-acre "sunken" property created by a sinkhole. Turner experimented with a variety of plants in the rich soil, eventually opening a nursery. By 1935, tours of his garden were so popular that he opened it to the public, charging a quarter for admission. Years later, the Turner family bought the Mediterranean-style building next door, creating "The World's Largest Gift Shop" as part of the Sunken Gardens attraction. Turner's exotic plants, flowers, and water features have captivated visitors for decades, establishing Sunken Gardens as one of Florida's favorite tourist destinations.

St. Petersburg Shuffleboard Club

1924–Present • St. Petersburg

"Our club was the first of its kind in the world . . . years ago the grandstands were packed. At the max, we had 107 courts being used. We had games being played on the courts from 8 in the morning until 10 in the evening. . . . It created a family out of people from everywhere. . . . The game itself is all accuracy and strategy. It's a lot like chess—the correct shot is not always the most obvious. It's a competitive battle. . . . St. Petersburg was the birthplace of land shuffleboard—it came from the ocean liners and then was adapted to land."* —Mary Eldridge, St. Petersburg Shuffleboard Club member since 1965

The world's largest and oldest shuffleboard club boasted over 100 courts and 5,000 members in its prime. Organized in 1924, the St. Petersburg Shuffleboard Club's membership included tournament-caliber players as well as those looking for a leisurely game. Special pride was taken in its top-ranked tournament players, now honored in the Shuffleboard Hall of Fame on the property. When not hitting the courts, members socialized at dances, bridge games, and movies at the downtown club.

Vinoy Park Hotel

1925–Present · St. Petersburg

"It was like a big family ... the guests arrived all at once to spend the winter months together. They came down with trunks full of gorgeous clothes and gorgeous jewels, and this was the time to wear them. . . . They would get all dolled up and take turns having cocktail parties. The men wore tuxedos. . . . They had afternoon tea and croquet on the front lawn. . . . These were wealthy people, well-heeled. The guests were always warm and gracious. To them, money was something they had always had."

—Lois Laughner Sullivan, daughter-in-law of Aymer Vinoy Laughner, founder of the Vinoy Park Hotel

The Roaring '20s romped through St. Petersburg, leaving behind lots of merrymaking—and the grandest hotel in city history. Florida's growth boom was in full force, and St. Petersburg was in need of a resort large and elegant enough to house its affluent northern visitors. In 1925, noted businessman Aymer Vinoy Laughner put up $3.5 million to build the luxurious 375-room Vinoy Park Hotel on the downtown waterfront, right across the street from his winter home. Its over-the-top Mediterranean architecture featured frescoed ceilings, ornamental plasterwork, pecky cypress beams, and an ornate observation tower. Celebrities and politicians came calling, including Babe Ruth, Herbert Hoover, and Jimmy Stewart.

Albert Whitted Airport

1928–Present • St. Petersburg

"I started out as an apprentice mechanic with National Airlines . . . (they) had a mail contract—that's how most early airlines got started. One of my odd jobs was carrying letters from a Model-A Ford mail truck to a National Airlines plane. I had to be armed—I guess it was a holdover from the Pony Express. . . . The location of this airport made it unique. Three of the four approaches were over water. I built a ramp and used a Cub on floats to instruct people how to fly seaplanes. They were the most fun to fly—you could go fishing or taxi right up to someone's house on the beach. You were only limited by your skill as a pilot. . . . Once, I built an amphibian out of the hull of a 14-foot fishing boat. And I've restored my share of 'basket cases'—that's a term for a plane that's in a lot of pieces!"* —Hank Palmer, retired pilot and mechanic whose relationship with St. Petersburg's Albert Whitted Airport began in 1937

"The birthplace of commercial aviation" is a big title for a little airport on St. Peterburg's downtown waterfront. What later became Albert Whitted Airport was the site of the take-off of the first scheduled commercial flight when, in 1914, a seaplane piloted by Tony Jannus and carrying one passenger skimmed out across the bay and set down in Tampa 23 minutes later. The modest, publicly owned airport, named after a well-liked local aviator, opened in 1928 and still operates today. It served National Airlines—one of the first air carriers in the country. It also housed the recognizable Goodyear Blimp for a short time before the Depression. During WWII, Albert Whitted Airport transformed into a military airfield where naval cadets took to the runways.

St. Petersburg Lawn Bowling Club

1917–Present · St. Petersburg

"*Every time I walked by the club, I saw everyone having such a good time. Finally, one day, I leaned over the fence and asked if I could join them. I've been a member ever since. . . . There were hundreds of bowlers in the early days. They came into town by bus and train and stayed at downtown hotels. . . . White was the thing to wear—we dressed in white trousers, shirts, and hats. . . . It's a gentle game. We bowled on a substance like a tennis court. When I tried bowling on grass, it took a lot more strength. . . . If your knees don't crack too badly, you'll do pretty well out here. . . . It's very friendly competition. Of course, you've got some serious players—I guess you've got to have them to spice it up a little.*"

—Ethel Vaughan, member of the St. Petersburg Lawn Bowling Club for over 25 years

It was Canadian "snowbird" Al Mercer who got the ball rolling on construction of Florida's oldest lawn bowling club. The city of St. Petersburg took up his cause, building a clubhouse, library, and rinks in 1917. There was just one problem: The grass used for bowling rinks wilted in Florida's heat, so Mercer suggested a synthetic clay rink—and the games began. The St. Petersburg Lawn Bowling Club hosted many competitions, including the first National Open Lawn Bowling Winter Tournament. During its peak years in the early 1950s, the club maintained 25 rinks for it's nearly 500 members.

Gulfport Casino

1935–Present · Gulfport

"*My fondest memories* were growing up around the waterfront—on Sunday, Wednesday, and Friday nights, there were big dances at the casino. When I was a kid, we stood outside, looked in the windows and watched. It was like being at the king's ball. Ladies had their hair done perfectly and wore beautiful old gowns. It was spectacular. . . . This was a quiet little town, but on those special nights, people came from all over. They bragged that the casino had the best dance floor—it was all hardwood oak. . . . The casino was also used for the town's fundraising events. The big attraction at the time was Chief Silver Tongue—he was an American Indian, a great vocalist. That's how we bought a new fire truck . . . . The casino has always been a gathering place for friendship and fun. It's still the crown jewel of Gulfport."*

—Bob Worthington, member of Gulfport's founding family

In the early 1900s, visitors eager to spend a day at the beach jumped a trolley to Gulfport's "electric pier," where they caught a boat to the Gulf beaches. This popular day trip put Gulfport on the map, and its first casino in business. While waiting for the ferry, tourists enjoyed entertainment, refreshments, and shopping at the pier's end. Soon, the casino pier complex became an attraction in itself. Two pavilions would come and go before the present day casino materialized in 1935 at the end of Beach Boulevard on the bay. The Gulfport Casino quickly became the social center of town, hosting everything from boxing matches to town meetings. But its well-worn wooden floor speaks volumes about the most popular activity in town—dancing the night away.

Bradenton Trailer Park

1936–Present · Bradenton

"It started out as a place for people vacationing with campers. . . . It was the largest park in the world—over a thousand lots. It was like a big, friendly family. Everyone cared for each other. . . . My parents came down here every season for 24 years. They enjoyed all the activities, especially shuffleboard and bible class. . . . At Christmas time, a group of us from Ohio got together and had a pot luck at the beach. We couldn't wait to tell everyone back home that our Christmas dinner was a picnic at the beach! We loved to show off our tans."*

—Martha Weaver, 30-year seasonal resident of Bradenton Trailer Park

Famous for having a palm tree on every lot, Bradenton Trailer Park lured vacationers looking for a place in the sun. Founded in 1936 by the local Kiwanis Club, the 46-acre property quickly earned the title "world's largest trailer park." Northerners eagerly headed south at the first sign of cold to enjoy Florida's glorious winters in the simple comfort of a mobile home. By the 1950s, the concept of retirement came of age, and Bradenton Trailer Park began catering to the over-60 crowd. As expected, retirees jumped at the chance to enjoy low-cost living with the benefit of Florida's easy-going lifestyle. The park complex bustled with an action-packed schedule of dances, shuffleboard, card games, and concerts.

N.E. Taylor Boatworks

1925–Present • Cortez

"*For two dollars* *you could pull your boat up on a cradle right underneath our house. . . . My dad would paint, repair, or build you a new boat. He built most of them out of cypress limbs from Perry or the Everglades. . . . Cypress was best because of the way it swelled up and absorbed water. . . . My dad and brothers would go hunting cedar timbers for the ribs—they went into the woods, swamps, and islands to find them . . . there were lots of mosquitoes and sand flies out there. . . . Sometimes, when our nets were out overnight, we slept on the roots of those mangroves, just to get off the water. . . . Whenever dad was planing boards for a new boat, girls from the neighborhood wanted the shavings, so they could put them in their hair like curls.*"

—Alcee Taylor, son of Neriah Elijah Taylor, who established N.E. Taylor Boatworks

Using simple building tools and cypress lumber harvested from the swamps, Neriah Taylor made a name for himself as a talented boat builder in the fishing village of Cortez. One of the town's early settlers, he built his home and workshop from hurricane driftwood scattered along Sarasota Bay. By 1925, N.E. Taylor Boatworks was in business, producing handcrafted wooden boats made of aged cypress and cedar timbers. A track running under the stilted workshop accommodated boats in need of repair. Whether building a pole skiff for navigating the bay's shallow waters or a "donkey" boat for pulling nets, Taylor did and still does provide a much-needed service for area fishermen and boaters.

Miakka School

1914–1944 • Miakka

"We had first grade through sixth in one room. We all got along well. . . . If you got punished for something you did at school, you got punished again when you got home. So we made sure we got along! . . . During the last year or two that I was there, we had a big wood-burning stove that was given to us by the Army. It was used in WWI. In the morning, everyone would bring in whatever they had—mostly vegetables—and we'd make a big pot of soup for lunch. . . . I lived three miles from school . . . one time we were walking home and we were playing around, throwing stuff at each other. I went off the dirt road to pick something up, and there was a rattlesnake, jarring its rattles at me . . . we ran the rest of the way home. That kept us back on the road from then on."*

—Fleta Carlton, native of Miakka and longtime cattle rancher who attended Miakka School during the early '30s

An iron bell signaled daybreak at Miakka School, where one teacher and up to fifty students hit the books. Without benefit of separate grades or a full school calendar, Miakka was typical of a rural 1914 schoolhouse. The only school within 30 miles, it ran a shortened five-month teaching schedule to accommodate hard-working farm families. Even "laundry day" was good reason for a day off. While school was in session, students' families shared their homes with the solitary teacher.

Arcadia All-Florida Championship Rodeo

1928–Present • Arcadia

"I thought I was smarter than mother and daddy and quit school in the eleventh grade. I went to work for the Circle Bar Cattle Company for $3 a week—including room and board. . . . In '48, I went on the road with Cherokee Hammon's Wild West Show. That's where I learned to rodeo. We started out in Key West and went all the way up to Canada. I rode buckin' horses and bulls . . . I never got hurt too seriously, just a broken leg or hand. . . . When I competed, I looked at it as a job. I took no chances. I went out there and did my best. . . . I was only five feet six and 165 pounds. Like any athlete, you've got to have drive and you've got to have heart."

—Runt Smith, Arcadia Rodeo All-Around Championship Cowboy 1949–51

When Arcadia's American Legion needed to hold a fundraiser to build a new hall, an unidentified club member and rancher Zeb Parker teamed up to take the bull by the horns. Both of them knew that cowboys lived for a little friendly competition with fellow ranch hands, so together they launched the first Arcadia All-Florida Championship Rodeo in 1928. It was so well received, it not only earned enough money for the American Legion hall, but also became an annual tradition that has lasted 80 years, making it the longest-running rodeo in the state. The participants in those first rodeos—most of whom were raised on nearby ranches—eagerly showed off hard-earned skills honed by years of cattle wrangling. Arcadia kicked off the main event with a crowd-pleasing rodeo parade through downtown.

DeSoto Palace Barber Shop

1913–Present • Arcadia

"I started out shining shoes at my father's barber shop down the street. . . . During the 1920s, people from the ranches came into town once a month on pay day. . . . The town was very busy back then—everything was right uptown. First, they stopped by the clothing store for a new shirt and pants. Then, they came in here to get a shower, shampoo, and shave. . . . I've heard you could even buy moonshine in the back. . . . Then, the guys went out and painted the town red. . . . Being friendly, good service, and a decent haircut—that's what has kept us going."

—Ed McClain, longtime barber and owner of DeSoto Palace Barber Shop

Known for its clean haircuts and close shaves, DeSoto Palace Barber Shop brought a touch of class to a rough-and-tumble ranching town in the early 1900s. Since 1926, three generations of the McClain family have served up haircuts, advice, and neighborhood news in the heart of DeSoto County. In Arcadia's early days, cowboys came into town for some much-needed grooming. Later, generations of townspeople received their first haircut and a sense of community at this downtown gathering place. Past owner Lonnie Walston tallied up a record 60 years of haircutting in DeSoto County.

Ringling Brothers and Barnum & Bailey Circus
Winter Quarters
1960–1992 · Venice

"*John Ringling North* *scouted the world to find the best performers. We were a little 'United Nations,' like a big family from all over. . . . We came home [to Venice] to rehearse before going back on the road in January to open a new season. There was always a lot of excitement coming into town. Everybody lined up to meet the train. . . . The performers and elephants headed across the bridge through town. It was tradition. . . . Sometimes we practiced in an empty lot near our home. Neighbors loved to bring over lawn chairs and watch. . . . I did a lot of tricks—the first quadruple somersault and a triple somersault—blindfolded. You're a kid. You enjoy the thrill. Who was scared? . . . To be in the center ring, you had to be the best. . . . Every moment of every single year was exciting.*"

—Tito Gaona, who began performing with the Ringling Brothers at age 14 as a member of the "Flying Gaonas—The First Family of the Air"

Even "The Greatest Show on Earth" needed time out of the spotlight. In 1960, after a non-stop 11-month tour, Ringling Brothers and Barnum & Bailey Circus headed south to recharge at its new winter quarters in Venice. After taking a well-deserved rest, circus artists spent days reinventing their acts for next season's shows. Acrobats, clowns, and animal trainers rehearsed in and out of arenas while enthusiastic townspeople served as their audience. Many performers, familiar with the area's mild winters and easygoing lifestyle, settled down in Venice upon retirement from the big top. Today, circus artist Tito Gaona runs a trapeze school on the grounds of the circus winter quarters.

Snook Haven Restaurant and Fish Camp

1948–Present · Venice

"I came out here as a customer before working here. You can't help but fall in love with this old place. It's another world out here. . . . People have always come for the river and the fishing. We didn't get our name, Snook Haven, for nothing. . . . When we first came out here, it was a pretty rough place. . . . At one time the cabins were used as a bordello. The ladies' names were still painted on the front of each door when we arrived. . . . At least two Tarzan movies were made here—one was called Tarzan and the Revenge of the Killer Turtles. *There's a legend that during filming, two of the killer turtles got loose and still roam the Myakka River! . . . We do know there is an 18-foot alligator out there. He looks like two big telephone poles strapped together. We call him 'Big Daddy.' "*

—Larry Cochrane, former general manager of Snook Haven

On the overgrown banks of the Myakka River, Snook Haven's cement block cabins once housed anglers ready to cast a line and relax. Located on the outskirts of Venice where a long dirt road dead ends at the river, Snook Haven officially opened for business in 1948. Before then, fishermen-in-the-know frequented the area without benefit of shelter. Snook Haven's colorful past included stints as a fish camp, a bordello, a movie set, and a "cracker-style" restaurant. Hollywood location scouts also discovered the raw beauty of the Myakka River, choosing it to as the backdrop for at least one *Tarzan* film. For over 50 years, its secluded setting and rustic character have provided a getaway from city life. Today, Snook Haven offers boat rentals, a restaurant, and a retreat house.

Warm Mineral Springs

North Port

"It was a relaxing place to work everyday—I came from the rapid pace and hustle bustle of northern cities. . . . Then, and now, it's the mineral water that attracts people. It has great qualities. In the early years, we collected testimonials and published them. . . . Even before my time, cowboys would stop by the spring to relax and heal their bodies after getting battered and bruised during cattle roundups. . . . Not long after WWII, servicemen who were wounded came here for relief. . . . It's like submersing your body in a warm solution of Epsom salts. The mineral content and flow of this water is higher than most springs in the world. . . . Many Europeans have come and gone through the years. They appreciate the minerals. Before they even get in the water, they know they're going to feel better."

—Sam Herron Jr., owner of Warm Mineral Springs from 1955–1999

Discoveries of well-preserved artifacts made Warm Mineral Springs one of the most significant underwater archaeological sites in America. But it was the spring's mineral-rich water that attracted people from all over the world. Convinced of the water's healing qualities, believers flocked to the spring for relief and relaxation. In fact, many still believe this is the site of Spanish explorer Ponce De Leon's legendary Fountain of Youth. Each day, nine million gallons of mineralized water rise up from a source 230 feet beneath the earth, making Warm Mineral the second-largest warm water spring in the western hemisphere.

Rainbow Springs

Dunnellon

"The Springs had a little bit of everything—a little ol' bathhouse, a place to get a drink, and a place to dance. . . . Kids came from all over. It's where we went for Sunday outings and family picnics. . . . When my husband was a boy, he and his friends paddled their homemade cypress boats down to the spring and camped out. There wasn't a bathing suit in sight! . . . Those days seem almost enchanted. . . . When the interstate came through Florida, it took traffic away from US 41 and Rainbow Springs. . . . An old friend who was back in town asked if I would take her down to the spring. After taking a long look, she said, 'When I get to heaven, I know it's got to be something like this.'"

—Ruth Riley, native of Dunnellon and author of *Memories of Rainbow Springs*

The free-flowing waters of Rainbow Springs drew inhabitants to it thousands of years ago. In the 1930s, developers hoped these same crystal-clear waters would work their magic on beach-weary tourists passing through the community of Dunnellon. Tourist attractions at Rainbow Springs offered landlubbers an underwater view of a first-magnitude Florida spring complete with fish and plant life—from the comfort of a partially submerged submarine boat. During the late '60s, the attraction expanded with a treetop monorail, a riverboat, and animal shows. Even though Rainbow Springs never reached the status of Silver Springs as a tourist destination, it was a favorite local spot for a Sunday picnic and a cool dip. Today's visitors enjoy swimming, picnicking, and camping at what is now Rainbow Springs State Park.

Ocala National Forest

1908–Present · Ocala

"People come out here to get away from the rush of everyday living. . . . In the forest, you're apt to see anything from an eagle to an alligator. There are also quite a few bears, but they're very secretive. I've had those special moments when I'm doing some trail work and there's no one around, but [I get the] feeling like something [is] there. . . . We get a lot of local people coming out here for guided tours. Quite often they're the children of pioneers who lived off this land, wanting to know more. . . . This is the land about which Marjorie Kinnan Rawlings wrote her book The Yearling. *She put this place on the map."*

—Johnnie Pohlers, native Floridian and forestry technician

Established in 1908, Ocala National Forest was once thought to be little more than a sand pine wasteland. But the variety of ecosystems that converge on this 400,000-acre expanse create a flourishing wildlife habitat and an outdoorsman's dream, not to mention the oldest national forest east of the Mississippi. Pine scrub, wetlands, oak hammocks, and flowing springs serve as a wilderness haven for a menagerie of beasts. These central Florida woodlands also served as home to early settlers determined to carve out a living in the wilderness between the St. John's River and the Ocklawaha. In the early 20th century, tourists and local residents enjoyed fishing, swimming, and hunting in the refuge of the forest. Today, it is one of the most heavily used national forests in the United States.

Lake Weir Yacht Club

1913–Present · East Lake Weir

"*In the early years,* people came across the lake in good, old-fashioned wooden launches to party at the club. . . . Northern visitors wintered in their homes around the lake. From New York Harbor, they came down on a steamer ship to Jacksonville. Then they took the train, which ran right past our front door at the club. . . . Dignitaries from Ocala also came in by train: the McKays, the Boyers, the Albrights. . . . I enjoyed the southern genteelness of the members. They came from all walks of life—politicians, grove owners, doctors, and judges. . . . We all dressed up for meetings and played bridge after dinner. It was a feeling of wonderful fellowship. . . . At the dinner table somebody would always call out, 'I'm not leaving until I have some of Gertie's potato salad or Karma's cheese grits!'*"

—Kathleen Wampola, member of the Lake Weir Yacht Club for more than 20 years

In Lake Weir Yacht Club's early years, Ocala's upper crust hopped a train to this rustic 1913 yacht club in Florida's central lake district for lakeside fun and late-night parties. Surrounded by hills planted in citrus, Lake Weir sponsored sailboat regattas and social gatherings for Ocala's elite, wealthy grove owners and lakeside winter residents. The party ended when the Seaboard Coast Line locomotive signaled its return trip to Ocala with a blow of its whistle.

Phillips Lake Weir Citrus

1930s–Present · Weirsdale

"It takes a certain amount of gamble and patience . . . we bought the grove when it was dead. It was killed by two freezes in consecutive winters. We had to wait five years before we had any fruit. . . . This piece of land has always been warmer—the winds come across the lake. And we're also on top of a hill—that keeps it three to four degrees warmer. . . . In the '30s, there was a railroad near the lake. Fruit was shipped across the lake on big barges and then hauled up north by train. . . . I enjoy working outside and growing something so valuable to people. We'll open up the windows and sell our fruit in bins right up front. . . . I like selling directly to the customer—you get to experience people tasting a product you've grown, enjoying it, and then taking it away."*

—Bill Phillips, former agricultural extension agent who established Phillips Lake Weir Citrus, on the site of a 1930s citrus grove in Marion County

Wild orange groves covered the hills and lake shores of central Marion County long before settlers made their livelihood from citrus. It is believed that early explorers brought the popular fruit from Spain, and Native Americans spread the seeds inland. Sandy soil, plenty of sun, and moderate temperatures contributed to the large number of successful groves around Lake Weir and Orange Lake—one of the oldest and most productive citrus regions in the state. Area grove owners shipped oranges by rail to northern cities in need of some Florida sunshine. A series of freezes in the 1890s put an end to many groves in Marion County and further north, pushing the citrus industry south. But some, like Phillips Lake Weir Citrus, flourished against the odds.

Sumter County Farmers Market

1937–Present • Webster

"I've been doing this since I was six years old. . . . It was easier years ago because there was an auction. We'd back the truck up into the market . . . buyers would bid on our whole lot of tomatoes. Then they'd ship it up north. People also did a lot more canning, so they bought more. By one o'clock, we were sold out. . . . All of us helped out at the market—aunts, uncles, and cousins. . . . Being farmers, we always had all you wanted to eat, and enough money left over to go to the drive-in once a week. We were happy. . . . I'm out in the fresh air, at least I'm not pushing a pencil."

—Bubba Stanley, native of Webster and lifelong truck farmer

Independent Sumter County farmers prepared their soil, planted their seed, and harvested their crops, but when it came time to market their produce, they needed a helping hand. In 1937, farmers from towns like Bushnell, Wildwood, and Webster joined forces, hiring an auctioneer to pump up the lagging price of produce. Working as a cooperative, Sumter County Farmers Market offered locally grown fruits and vegetables in bulk to the highest bidder. This method of selling became so successful that a livestock auction and flea market followed. Buyers scheduled their week's shopping around Webster's farmers' market, where they could buy anything from an old tractor to a bushel of green beans.

Mount Dora A.C.L. Railroad Station

1915–1973 · Mount Dora

"I lived a couple blocks from the depot. Trains used to come through here, blowing their whistle. It sure woke you up! . . . The tourists from up north came in from Sanford on the train and headed over to the Lakeside Inn—only the wealthy stayed there. . . . Not that many people traveled by automobile back then, so they came in by train. They stayed two to three months, enjoying the good old sunshine. . . . We used to ship a lot of fruit on the railroad, before trucking took over. Lumber came into town the same way. . . . The train was just part of everyday living."*

—Dorothy Tremain, member of one of Mount Dora's
founding families and resident since 1929

Mount Dora became a central-Florida destination when train service made its way to this quiet lakeside community in 1886. Both cargo and passengers moved on the rail line between Tampa and Jacksonville. While northern sportsmen caught the train south to Mount Dora for fishing and boating getaways, local citrus growers used the train to ship their prized fruit north. Built in 1915, the Atlantic Coast Line Railroad depot served as an arrival station for guests visiting Mount Dora's elegant Lakeside Inn. A porter greeted guests as they stepped off the train and then hauled their luggage to the high-end resort. The Mount Dora Chamber of Commerce is currently housed in the train depot and remains a center of activity for visitors and residents.

Daytona Beach Band Shell

1937–Present • Daytona Beach

"We rented a funny, old beach cottage on Ocean Avenue
. . . . *The band shell was the center of social activity on the beachside—everybody would go to the boardwalk and listen to the bands.
There was always something going on . . . children put on dance
shows, beauty pageants were held . . . we practically lived down there
in the summertime. . . . People came from small central Florida
towns because it was cooler over here in the summer. . . . The band
shell is one of a kind. It's made of coquina—that's what the fort in
St. Augustine is made of. It lasts forever. . . . There's nothing prettier
than looking out at the ocean from the band shell."*

—Mary Luellen, native Floridian and Daytona Beach resident since 1922

When the Daytona Beach Band Shell sprang to life on July 4, 1937, it jumpstarted an era of entertainment on the oceanfront. The state-of-the-art boardwalk band
shell arrived in style with a parade, a concert, and the crowning of Miss Daytona
Beach. Built of coquina rock—a mixture of broken shells and coral—this beachside
amphitheatre boasted excellent acoustics and seating for 4,000. From its simple
beginnings as a Depression-era federal project, it became one of Daytona Beach's
most cherished landmarks. A parade of concerts and special events continues to
draw residents and visitors to the heart of Daytona Beach.

Stamie's Swimwear and the Jantzen Girl

1945–Present • Daytona Beach

"When Europeans who don't speak a word of *English saw the Jantzen girl, they instantly knew there were swim-suits inside. She's one of only three in the world. . . . Originally, I wanted to put her out on the pier as an advertisement, but I was warned she would blow away with the first storm. . . . In the old days, people wanted service. I loved pleasing my customers, fitting them properly and making them happy. We were like family. . . . When Daytona became the 'in' place for students, things got out of control. That's about the time bikinis came in fashion. At first, some of my customers were afraid to wear them. . . . We also carried fine hand-made dresses—people dressed up to go out back then, furs and all."*

—Stamie Kypreos, owner of Stamie's Swimwear

The Jantzen girl almost ended up in hot water when the Miami business originally showcasing the model closed for good. Swim shop owner Stamie Kypreos came to the rescue, perching the recognizable red-suited model on Stamie's Swimwears' rooftop in Daytona Beach. Located on Ocean Avenue just off the boardwalk since 1945, Stamie's witnessed the evolution of beach wear from full-coverage suits to string bikinis. The Jantzen girl symbol traces its roots back to the 1920s, when Jantzen introduced "The Suit That Changed Bathing to Swimming."

Zeno's Candies

1948–Present • Daytona Beach

"Uncle Tom brought my husband over from Greece in 1954 and taught him the candy-making trade. . . . All our chocolates are hand dipped, piece by piece. It takes hours of practice to get the right touch. . . . In the beginning, we only had taffy and fudge because we didn't have air conditioning. . . . Our taffy puller is the original machine his uncle started the business with. He purchased it from Coney Island in 1916. It's been running ever since. . . . Some customers tell us they're not allowed to go home unless they bring back our salt water taffy. . . . People are the best thing about this business. . . . Our customers used to watch the taffy puller through the window when they were kids—and now they're back with their grandkids."*

—Joyce Louizes, wife of Zeno Louizes, owner of Zeno's Candies

An almost century-old taffy-pulling machine marked the spot where diets ended and vacations began. Just steps from Daytona Beach, Zeno's Candies enticed the boardwalk crowd with its made-from-scratch candies—especially saltwater taffy, the definitive beach treat. Ice cream and fudge rounded out the kid-inspired menu. Since 1948, three generations of the Louizes family have fine-tuned their candy making skills, welcoming customers to watch the show through their large picture window on Main Street.

Ponce De Leon Inlet Light Station

1887–Present • Ponce Inlet

"*I remember when boats would wreck in the inlet. They would beach themselves because it was so treacherous. Sometimes they would get caught in a storm. . . . My father and his assistants rescued the people and my mother would feed and clothe them. My job was to help mom. . . . My family lived on the grounds along with two assistant keepers. We always had friends to play with because the assistant keepers had children, too. Whenever we played a game, there were enough of us to make up our own teams! . . . When the war started, they moved our family out, and Coast Guard personnel moved in.*"

—Gladys Davis, daughter of Edward L. Meyer, head lighthouse keeper at Ponce De Leon Inlet Light Station from 1937–43

The dangerous shoals and deceptive currents of Ponce Inlet gave rise to the tallest lighthouse in Florida history. Soaring 175 feet in the air, Ponce De Leon Inlet Light Station came to life in 1887 with the help of a kerosene lamp in a Fresnel lens (an efficient lens used to concentrate and project light). The brick fortress served as both navigational aid and warning beacon for Atlantic mariners off the coast of Daytona Beach. In the early days, keepers climbed 203 steps to clean the lens, trim the wick, and, most importantly, keep the light burning. The introduction of electricity made the keeper's job less demanding, and by 1953 the Ponce Inlet Lighthouse was totally self-supporting.

Athens Theatre

1922–Present • DeLand

"It was the best time to grow up, during the Depression. You didn't know you were poor. Everyone else was poor, too. . . . The theatre was our only form of entertainment. On Saturday afternoons all the kids in town would scrape up nine cents and go to the movies. The first movie I ever saw was a silent one. I was only six years old and couldn't even read the subtitles. . . . I'll never forget the disappointment when I saw The Hunchback of Notre Dame—*I thought it was a football movie! . . . Stage shows also came through town. I remember Sally Rand, the fan dancer. . . . During the late '30s and '40s, I carried my dates to the Athens. We called the balcony 'the passion pit!' "*

—Bill Dreggors, fourth-generation Floridian and lifelong DeLand resident

When it was established in 1922, the Athens Theatre became the Carnegie Hall of Volusia County. Destined to be the star of DeLand, the Athens featured state-of-the-art design, construction, and equipment. Silent movies and vaudeville acts entertained the earliest crowds, followed by touring stage shows, talent contests, and first-run movies. Seating accommodated 500 people, and a Wurlitzer pipe organ provided the musical backdrop for performances large and small. For more than half a century, family social calendars hinged on the latest event at the Athens.

Cassadaga Spiritualist Camp

1894–Present · Cassadaga

"Everybody who lives here is a Spiritualist—we believe in the continuity of life and reincarnation. . . . Everyone who comes on these grounds speaks of a feeling of serenity, a special vibration. . . . When my husband and I moved down here in 1948, Cassadaga was a winter camp for Spiritualists. After he became president of the camp, it became year-round. . . . I've been teaching natural laws and the part they play in our lives since 1953. . . . A medium has developed the insight and ability to tune into people. Like any talent, you have to put your heart into it. When we intellectualize, we get confused. . . . Whenever I give a reading to someone, I feel like I'm answering some need of theirs. I tune into their turmoil."

—Eloise Page, Spiritualist teacher, lecturer,
and medium at Cassadaga Spiritualist Camp

In 1875, with a Native American spirit as his guide, medium George Colby pinpointed the woodlands of central Florida as the ideal place to set up a camp for his fellow Spiritualists. Established in 1894, Cassadaga Spiritualist Camp welcomed all Spiritualists, including those who practiced their belief in communicating with the spirit world. Clapboard cottages replaced tents as Cassadaga evolved from a winter retreat for northern Spiritualists into the year-round religious community that it is today, where residents own their homes, but not the land.

Little Drug Company

1920–Present · New Smyrna Beach

"Every morning we'd have four to six regulars waiting at the door when we opened. We had the 'coffee clutchers,' and then we had those who wanted breakfast. . . . We still have a full running fountain and restaurant. Our milkshakes are made-to-order. Some say our hamburgers have always been the best in town—I can tell you the grill is well seasoned. . . . We compound most prescriptions ourselves and, if you like, we deliver them to your door. . . . On Saturday afternoon, we've always closed at two o'clock . . . New Smyrna rolls up the sidewalk early. That's tradition around here."*

—Skip Barnes, general manager of Little Drug Company for over 25 years

In the early '20s, Little Drug Company began serving up a healthy dose of sundries, sodas, and sundaes for New Smyrna Beach residents. Housed in the old Victoria Theatre building, Little Drug made its mark with over-the-top customer service and a dedicated staff, not to mention their soda fountain and grill. Whether in the form of a prescription or a friendly chat, this main street drug store delivered. Celebrating over 85 years in business, Little Drug is the oldest ongoing independent drug store in Volusia County.

Hale Indian River Groves

1947–Present • Wabasso

"Dad started off from scratch with a roadside *stand. That's how he got most of his customers. . . . People came down from up north and hauled bags of fruit back home. As a child, I carried fruit out to their car or poured them a cup of orange juice. . . . It was busy—I was paid one cent for each quarter bushel I bagged. . . . Fruit shipping has always been the main part of our business. . . . Navels and grapefruit were the most popular, especially at Christmas time. . . . My dad was innovative and didn't mind trying new ways to get business. He used mailing lists and direct mail catalogs to reach customers everywhere."*

—Steve Hale III, son of Steve Hale Jr., who established Hale Groves

Winter tourists liked nothing better than sharing a bag of Florida oranges with friends and family up north. In 1947, from his roadside stand in the heart of the Indian River Citrus Belt, Steve Hale found an easier way for his customers to share the sunshine: mail order. Hale and his family picked, packed, and shipped oranges and grapefruit to an ever-growing list of mail-order customers while continuing to serve drive-up visitors. A family-operated business for over half a century, Hale Groves grew from a one-man fruit stand into one of the state's top mail-order fruit shipping companies.

Desert Inn at Yeehaw Junction

1880s–Present • Yeehaw Junction

"Anybody and everybody who traveled down SR 60 or US 441 going north, south, east, or west passed by here. . . . The reason traders used to track through here was because these were the high roads. This area was mostly underwater—the highest ground became the road. . . . Trucking companies used to call, looking for their drivers. They would say, 'We know you're taking a break there —now get back on the road!' . . . There were a lot of cowboys around early on. One of the previous owners would hand them a cold beer right in the saddle. That's called a 'beer to go!' . . . Today, everybody says, 'Get it to me quick, whatever it is.' . . . Here, everything is home-cooked."*

—Beverly Ziecheck, longtime owner of the Desert Inn

Like an oasis in the Sahara, the Desert Inn has beckoned the tired, the thirsty, and the hungry for more than 75 years. Rising from the crossroads of US 441 and SR 60— otherwise known as Yeehaw Junction—the inn has worn many hats since the early 1900s, including that of trading post, watering hole, and brothel. Whether you were a cowboy driving cattle south or a trucker in need of rest, the Desert Inn was a welcome sight midst the lonely lowlands north of Lake Okeechobee. Today, it's a down-home restaurant and no-frills hotel.

Holman Stadium

1953–Present • Vero Beach

"I was born less than 500 feet from home plate—[the stadium grounds] used to be the naval air force hospital during WWII. . . . At Homan Stadium, you got closer to the players. It was homey. . . . You had open dugouts, so you might be sitting in the first row and literally hear what went wrong in the last inning. . . . I was batboy the day Sandy Koufax broke into baseball. . . . I've shagged balls for Duke Snider. . . . Players came from every walk of life. Some were big brutes. Some were kind. But they all had the same dream of getting into the big leagues. They weren't paid well or pampered. They did it for the love of the game." —Chet Hogan, born and raised in Vero Beach

The grounds of a vacant naval air base became home to cracking bats and flying baseballs when the Brooklyn Dodgers landed in Vero Beach. Brought to town by local entrepreneur Bud Holman in 1953, the Dodgers began conducting spring training at a former military base complex dubbed "Dodgertown," the only privately owned training camp in the country. Holman Stadium continues to offer baseball enthusiasts a privileged look at a major league team in training. With its open-air dugouts and cozy seating, this uncluttered stadium provides spectators with an up-close view of famous players and raw action. For over 50 years, the Dodgers have come to Vero Beach to dust off their bats for a new season of baseball.

The Highwaymen

1950s–1970s • Fort Pierce, Melbourne, Vero Beach, West Palm Beach, Stuart

"The three of us painted together. We were friends—Alfred Hair, Harold Newton, and me. One was the fastest painter, one the better painter, and I knew how to sell a painting. . . . We all wanted the same things—a nice car and a home. We were very competitive, though. If Alfred said he was going to paint half a day, I would paint all day! . . . We had to go to the people. We drove to Vero Beach, Stuart, Palm Beach, Cocoa, and Melbourne. . . . We sold our paintings in the morning, and then drove back and painted some more. . . . Tourists came down, bought a painting, and took it back as a souvenir. You weren't a Floridian until you had a palm tree, water, and a sunset. . . . When tourists went back up north, the weather was cold, and the oranges and reds in our paintings made them feel warm inside."

—James Gibson, Florida landscape painter and member of "The Highwaymen"

Their car trunks loaded with freshly painted pictures, a group of African-American artists from Fort Pierce took to the streets to sell their wares. Traveling up and down the Treasure Coast of southeast Florida, they successfully peddled their paintings to businessmen and tourists from the late '50s through the '70s. Noted Florida landscape artist A.E. Backus acted as mentor to these ambitious young painters who were determined to make a better living in the segregated South. With hard work and a creative eye, they acquired their own "quick style" of painting based on an idealized image of the Florida landscape. Since low overhead costs and brisk sales were essential to their livelihood, "The Highwaymen" marketed their colorful artwork on foot, stopping by doctors offices, banks, restaurants, and even the side of the road.

Adams Ranch

1937–Present • Fort Pierce

"It's everybody's dream as a kid—having a horse, a gun, working cattle, and hunting. . . . By '42, most of the young men had gone to war. All that was left were the older men and boys like myself. I was 15 when we drove cattle across state on horseback. . . . Swimming cattle across the Kissimmee River was the most fun. We got the job done as good as anybody. . . . This kind of work is just too hard to do, if you really don't like it. . . . Old time cattlemen were free ranging in this area, but my father foresaw the end of the open range. He realized you had to buy the land, fence it, and pay taxes. . . . This is cattle ranching in its purest form—we have flat land, sunshine, and no worries about putting up hay or feed."

—Alto "Bud" Adams Jr., son of Alto Adams Sr., who established Adams Ranch

When Florida's Supreme Court was not in session, Justice Alto Adams Sr. pulled on a pair of boots and headed for his ranch near Fort Pierce. Little did he know his small tract of land purchased in 1937 would grow into a family cattle ranch encompassing 65,000 acres in three counties—one of the largest in the country. His son, Alto "Bud" Adams, led the way in adapting cattle to south Florida's unique environment. Adams' Braford breed was specifically developed to tolerate heat, humidity, and insects. Celebrated for its environmental stewardship, Adams Ranch continues to manage its land in balance with nature. Its oak hammocks, grasslands, and ponds are home to deer, alligators, bobcats, and a variety of bird life.

Okeechobee Livestock Market

1937–Present • Okeechobee

"We're out in the middle of cow country—we're the second-largest livestock market east of the Mississippi. . . . Our calves go out all over the country. People like these Florida calves. They figure if they can stand the heat, humidity, and bugs, they ought to do good anywhere. . . . Back when this was a dirt road, they would drive in cattle with horses instead of trucks. . . . Auction day was unique. It had its own smell and noise—we took in cattle at 7:30 a.m. and kept going until they were gone. . . . I'll never forget our first sale of 1,000 head—we didn't know if we could handle that many. . . . We've been in the cattle business all our lives, these people are our friends and neighbors—you treat them right."*

—Pete Clemons, owner of Okeechobee Livestock Market since 1961

Scrawny scrub cows roamed Florida's wilderness long before cattle ranching became one of the state's leading industries. With time, the quality of cattle improved, and as the need for pasture increased, the cattle industry moved farther south into Okeechobee County. A central stockyard for buying and selling cattle became essential. In 1937, the local Cattlemen's Association opened Okeechobee Livestock Market, where auctions drew in buyers and sellers from around the region. Owned by the Clemons family since 1961, Okeechobee Livestock Market is the largest volume market in Florida.

Boca Grande Lighthouse

1890–Present · Boca Grande, Gasparilla Island

"We moved to the lighthouse when I was three . . . I looked up at that big place with all those steps and thought I was in heaven. . . . We had such freedom. We fished, we shelled, we climbed trees. We wore no shoes to school and went swimming for P.E. I didn't realize that everyone's childhood was not like mine. . . . In the winter, when tourists came down to the beach, I sold them seashells—I even had a display case. Other days, I walked down to the dock and decided what kind of fish I wanted to catch that day. . . . I watched ships come in from all over, getting phosphate for fertilizer. . . . We moved away when I was 13—I hugged all the pillars when we left."*

—Dian D. Miller, daughter of Cody W. McKeithen,
Boca Grande Lighthouse keeper from 1941–51

Standing at just 44 feet tall on a series of iron pilings, the Boca Grande Lighthouse guided seafaring freighters through the deep waters of Boca Grande Pass into its port. In the late 1800s, dock workers at the port were busy loading Florida's newest commodity—phosphate. In 1890 when the lighthouse was built, demand for phosphate-based fertilizer was high and Florida seemed to have an endless supply. Barges loaded with phosphate traveled down the Peace River into Charlotte Harbor and unloaded at Port Boca Grande. As cargo ship traffic increased through the channel, so did the importance of the Boca Grande Lighthouse. Perched on the southern tip of Gasparilla Island, this wood-frame lighthouse remained in the spotlight until the bigger and better-equipped port of Tampa came of age decades later.

Shiloh Baptist Church

1959–1984 • Boca Grande, Gasparilla Island

"Our congregation was made up of about 40 people . . . some worked on the phosphate docks, some were groundskeepers. Others were maids and cooks. . . . The church was primarily a gathering place—it was the only building large enough. The Methodists had their services on the first and third Sundays, and the Baptists on the second and fourth Sundays. We supported one another. That's what kept us going. . . . One time, during high tide, a storm came up—we had fair warning. When the water receded we had to shovel out the sand and let the church dry out. But the Lord was with us—in a few weeks we got everything back to normal. . . . Before there was a bridge to Boca Grande, this was a close-knit community, black and white. Everybody knew everybody. Nobody locked doors. . . . When I look back, I can be proud of living through a time like that." —Thomas Philpot, former deacon of Shiloh Baptist Church

Beginning in the early 1900s, African-Americans worked on the phosphate docks and at the homes of seasonal Boca Grande residents. Despite the fact that these African-Americans were longtime residents of Boca Grande, their community was relocated to make way for downtown development in the late '50s. Although another neighborhood was developed for them on the south side of Gasparilla Island, it was without a place of worship, and their churches in Boca Grande were razed in the redevelopment. Winter resident Roger Amory took action, arranging the construction of a chapel to be shared by both the Baptist and Methodist congregations of the black community. Set on the dunes of Boca Grande, Shiloh Baptist Church served as a neighborhood gathering place as well as a joint venture in religion.

Whidden's Marina

1926–Present • Boca Grande, Gasparilla Island

"It was the friendliest place in town. *All the guides, at one time or another, ended up there. . . . Captain Sam would run a tab for us fishermen—he would let us pay him whenever we got the money. . . . It was more or less a local's place. . . . Everyone else updates and renovates, but not there. What you see today is what you saw yesterday. . . . I remember one day when I was a young man, standing in line with a basketful of groceries from the marina store. The guy behind me asked Sam if he could go ahead of me because he was in a hurry. Sam answered, saying, 'No—if you were in such a hurry, you should have gotten here 20 minutes ago!' Sam either liked you or he didn't."*

—Cappy Joiner, third-generation tarpon fishing guide and
founding member of the Boca Grande Fishing Guides Association

Sitting on the calm waters of Boca Bayou, Whidden's Marina was home away from home for hard-working fishing guides. Friendly competition combined with owner Sam Whidden's hospitality made Whidden's a comfortable headquarters for guides and serious fishermen alike. Boca Grande's reputation for out-of-this-world Tarpon fishing has kept guides on their toes and Whidden's Marina hopping for over 75 years. Family owned and operated since 1926, Whidden's also made its mark as a local's hangout and once included a restaurant and dance hall.

Pineland Post Office

1925–Present • Pineland, Pine Island

"*The post office* *was more or less a community center, a place to visit neighbors, to sit and exchange news and gossip. . . . Before bridges were built, boats ran from Punta Gorda to the islands. In Pineland, there was a long dock that went way out because it was so shallow. If it was low tide, the postmistress had to wade out and bring sacks of mail ashore. She also had to carry the outgoing mail. . . . Passengers who caught a ride on the mail boat would be all dressed up in long dresses and stockings. They also had to walk in to shore. . . . Back then, buildings like the post office were built loosely, so winds could pass through. They swayed and creaked, but they could withstand a hurricane.*"

—Elaine Blohm Jordan, author and former editor of the *Pine Island Eagle* newspaper

After Pineland's first attempt at an official post office washed away, postmistress Ruby Gill took the reins. In 1925, when stamps cost just three cents, she built the tiny Pineland Post Office for $200—and continued to tend her orange groves and gladiolas. Located among Native American shell mounds on secluded Pine Island, the clapboard post office served about 40 residents in this island community, where mail traveled by boat. After retiring 32 years later, Ruby proudly recalled the boat missing only one mail pickup, due to a hurricane. Until 1955, Ruby and the U.S. Postal Service relied upon a verbal agreement for mail service, with no official contract.

Sunburst Tropical Fruit Company

1920–Present • Bokeelia, Pine Island

"They had a severe freeze in 1915—it was devastating. . . . Mr. Harry Poe Johnson, the first owner [of Sunburst], said he was going to find a spot not whacked by the freeze. I think he made a pretty good choice. . . . The trees went in around 1920, and I still have most of the original trees. . . . Back then, clearing the land was done with mules and day laborers—fires and chains. It was slow going. This island was covered with big stands of pines. . . . In the late '40s, the second owner, Dr. Peterson, shipped fruit all over the country. His wife was his right-hand person. . . . It's funny how we've ended up going down that same path. My wife is the one who got the kitchen started up again and began canning mango preserves and chutney. . . . Now, we're mostly a mail-order business, just like years ago.' "*

—Gary Crochowski, native Floridian and
longtime owner of Sunburst Tropical Fruit Company

Pine Island's livelihood had always come from the sea. But in the early 1900s, a new breed of settler tried its hand at cultivating the land. Between storms and freezes, pioneers experimented with raising a variety of fruits, including mango and avocado. The groves of Sunburst Tropical Fruit Company date back to those first plantings. Hands down, it was the taste and hardiness of the Pine Island mango that stood above the rest. By 1920, Pine Island mangos were in demand across the country. Sunburst Tropical Fruit Company, along with other early groves, kept mothers and daughters busy canning and shipping orders. Today, Pine Island is home to a thriving tropical fruit industry, offering delicacies such as papaya, carambola, and loquat.

Bokeelia Pier

1904–Present • Bokeelia, Pine Island

"Our family homestead was here—my dad came in 1917. He had a nursery with avocado trees. . . . Bokeelia had a general store, post office, and small hotel. . . . In the summertime we would go swimming off the dock. It was the Howard boys and us. . . . The dock has been rebuilt several times because of storms, but it's the original location of the Punta Gorda Fish Company. . . . Out on the end of the dock there was a little house where the tender of the fish house stayed. There was an icehouse, too. . . . The boat came down from Punta Gorda with ice and then continued on down the sound. When it came back the next day, the boat picked up fish—mostly mullet—that was brought in by our fishermen."

—Vince Honc, born and raised in Bokeelia

Pirates roamed Bokeelia's secluded shores long before Pine Island was discovered by homesteaders in the late 1800s. Just like the Native Americans and Spanish before them, these buccaneers frequented the northern tip of Pine Island because of its ideal location and bountiful waters. In 1904, Bokeelia's first permanent residents built a pier stretching out into Charlotte Harbor where "run boats" picked up and delivered mail, supplies, and passengers. Later, a fish house topped off the pier, providing area fishermen with a place to transport their catch to market. Although Pine Island lacked Florida's typical sandy beaches, Bokeelia's shallow waterfront was the perfect setting for community picnics, fish fries, and get-togethers.

Shell Factory

1938–Present • North Fort Myers

"We had it all: shells, resort wear, moccasins, and a big jewelry room. . . . A favorite was 'pick a pearl.' We would take an oyster, open it, clean it up, and make a necklace or earrings out of it. . . . People bought baskets full of shells, and we had to know the name and price of every one of them. There were bins of different shells running the length of the store. . . . I used to like the little sea urchin with a bulb in it. They even made floral arrangements out of shells. . . . Collectors came in looking for very rare shells—one was worth a couple thousand dollars. . . . I liked my job so much, I never wanted a day off . . . I met people from all over the world."*

—Gloria Clemente, retired Shell Factory salesperson

Evolving from a neighborhood shell stand in Bonita Springs to a sprawling souvenir warehouse on US 41 in Fort Myers, the Shell Factory catered to tourists eager to bring home a piece of the beach. Not only did the store carry every kind of shell, sponge, and fossil imaginable; it sold kitschy accessories made from shells, including lamps, wind chimes, and hotplates. Since 1938, the Shell Factory has survived a number of challenges, including fires, a hurricane, relocations, and rerouted traffic. In 2008, the Shell Factory celebrated 70 years as the top souvenir mecca on Florida's southwest coast.

Clewiston Inn

1926–Present • Clewiston

"All the advantages we had in this town were given to us by the sugar company—including the inn. It was the social center of town. Everything was held there—weddings, reunions, any important social event. . . . It was known for its southern food and hospitality. My mother worked there as a hostess and remembers people driving all the way up from Miami for their southern buffet. Everybody in town favored it, too. . . . The Royal Air Force trained near here during WWII, and they still have reunions at the inn—they said they'd never forget the hospitality of the people of Clewiston."

—Frances Nall, Clewiston resident since 1930

In its early days, the Clewiston Inn—located smack in the middle of sugar cane country, between Lake Okeechobee and the Everglades—delivered a genteel touch to a town born of the sugar industry. In 1926, the hotel was built for the sole purpose of hosting U.S. Sugar Corporation executives, dignitaries, and guests. Clewiston locals also became regulars for social events in this remote town surrounded by cane fields. A fire destroyed the original lodge, but the Clewiston Inn was rebuilt in the Colonial Revival style in 1938, adding a touch of southern charm to "the sweetest town in America." A hand-painted mural of the Everglades encircles its popular lounge, where sugar executives, visitors, and townspeople gather.

Big Cypress Seminole Reservation

1933–Present · Hendry County

"I grew up in the woods. When I was a child, we ran through the swamps and swam in the rivers and lakes. We weren't afraid of anything. . . . Every day I went into the woods and picked up firewood—we always kept a fire burning. . . . Canoes were our only transportation, like today's car. It was used for hunting and fishing. And some days the whole family would get in and go visiting relatives. We carried cabbage fronds to fan the children. . . . My father traded hides, coon, and deer. And sometimes, white men asked him to guide them through the swamps."*

—Ingram Billie Jr., born and raised in a Seminole camp, member of the Wind Clan

As many as 100,000 Native Americans called Florida home during the 1500s. But after years of war, disease, and banishment, little remained of Florida's American Indian population. By the mid-1800s, only about 500 members of the Seminole tribe persevered, disappearing into the tangled swamps and maze-like wetlands of the Everglades. When the Seminoles emerged years later, they traded goods, worked the land, and sold crafts. In 1957, tribal members adopted their own constitution, officially establishing themselves as the Seminole Tribe of Florida. Big Cypress is the largest of five Seminole reservations in the state, covering some 50,000 acres from Lake Okeechobee to Alligator Alley.

Naples Pier

1888–Present · Naples

"*Naples was so quiet back then,* *you almost never saw a car. . . . We lived a couple blocks from the pier. I used to get up before school and swim to the end of it. At the time, I thought it was a lovely thing to do. . . . An old sign was recently found—it read, 'Please don't throw fish on the dance floor.' It was posted because every Saturday night, the end of the pier was turned into a dance floor—I guess they didn't want anyone slipping! . . . People have always been drawn to the pier. Through the years, newer residents would go [there] to meet people. Even people who have lived here for years would take a stroll after dinner. . . . It's a very romantic place as well, with the moon and stars.*"

—Jackie Frank, Naples resident since 1949

Surrounded by wilderness swamp on one side and the Gulf of Mexico on the other, Naples received everyone and everything by water. The 600-foot-long Naples Pier, one of the town's original structures, welcomed steamships full of supplies, vacationers, and settlers. When it was built in 1888, this T-shaped wooden pier was Naples' only connection to the outside world. Heavy freight and passenger luggage was transported by a simple tramway down the pier to the only building in town: the hotel. Rebuilt several times due to hurricanes and fire, the Naples Pier remains the center of this beachside community.

Rod and Gun Club

1922–Present · Everglades City

"*People came here* *from all over the world to go fishing. I remember seeing celebrities slipping in and out of town. . . . The old guide boats would tie up at the dock in front of the club to load up for a day's fishing. There were so many boats, they reached down to the curve in the river. . . . The wait staff would come out with big wicker baskets full of fresh fruit, cold cuts, linens, and silver—everything needed to go out fishing for the day. . . . I helped my brother deliver 300-pound blocks of ice to the box near the club's kitchen. Guides also got a big block of ice for their fish box. . . . The Rod and Gun Club is like stepping back in time—when you walk out the door, you think you're going to see Josie Billie in a dugout canoe.*"

—Bob Wells, third-generation resident of the Everglades City area

If you were a friend of Florida land magnate Baron Collier, you just might have been invited to a sporting getaway at his private club on the border of the Everglades. In 1922, Collier purchased the Rod and Gun Club, located on what was once the site of a wilderness trading post, for the purpose of entertaining his wealthy northern guests. Yet untamed, the western boundary of the Everglades offered abundant wildlife and seclusion for the avid sportsman. Later, Collier put Everglades City on the map with construction of the Tamiami Trail through the Everglades wilderness. Hunting and fishing trophies still line the cypress-paneled walls of the lodge where five presidents and a slew of celebrities unwound.

Smallwood Store

1906–1982 · Chokoloskee Island

"Smallwood's was the hub of the community. It had all the supplies you needed. . . . Before 1956, everything was brought in by boat. There was no road to the island. . . . This was a pretty lawless area. If you came down here, you were probably running from the law. . . . My grandfather played postmaster and doctor—he became a trusted friend to the Indians. Some came all the way from the east coast to deal with him because they knew he would treat them fairly. . . . In the early years, Indians came at Christmastime and camped beside the store. They brought hides, fresh meat, pelts, and wild turkey. . . . Many of the elders in the tribe remember my grandfather as the first white man they ever saw."

—Lynn Smallwood McMillin, granddaughter of Ted Smallwood,
founder of Smallwood Store

In 1906, Smallwood Store was the equivalent to the modern-day convenience store—on stilts. Located on remote, newly settled Chokoloskee Island just west of the Everglades, Smallwood's served the everyday needs of pioneer families who farmed, fished, and hunted. The stilts gave the store a special look, but what made Smallwood's truly unique was its reputation as a Native American trading post. At a time when most Native Americans considered white men untrustworthy, proprietor Ted Smallwood became a trusted friend of the Seminoles, trading hides and furs with them. A jack-of-all-trades, Smallwood moved easily between the jobs of postmaster, trader, merchant, and peacemaker. Smallwood Store currently operates as a living museum of pioneer history.

Gilbert's Bar House of Refuge

1876–1945 • Stuart, Hutchinson Island

"I had a friend named Shirley Culpepper . . . her father was in charge of the Coast Guard station [Gilbert's Bar House of Refuge]. Her whole family lived there—it was just home to them. Mr. Culpepper had certain obligations though: He would scan the ocean for any signs of distress. He had enlisted men under him to help with other duties. . . . When I spent the night with Shirley, we slept in the sleeping bay on the second floor. . . . The waves crashed on the rocks in front of the house every few minutes. The ocean made so much noise, I couldn't sleep all night. Shirley was used to it. . . . During WWII, the observation tower was used to spot enemy boats and planes. I used to talk to the enlisted men in the tower—my mother wouldn't let me talk with them by phone for more than 10 minutes."*

—Anita Tilton Wacha, born and raised on Hutchinson Island

If you were one of the lucky survivors of a shipwreck off Florida's east coast, help was just down the beach. Perched on the rocky shoreline of Hutchinson Island, the men of Gilbert's Bar House of Refuge and the U.S. Life Saving Service stood ready to aid storm-tossed sailors rescued from the Atlantic's rough seas and shoals. Built in 1876, it was one of ten life-saving shelters welcoming the lost and weary along Florida's treacherous coast. Keepers and their families lived in the main quarters, while rescued sailors settled into an upstairs dormitory. In 1915, the U.S. Life Saving Service merged with the Coast Guard. During WWII, coastguardsmen stationed at Gilbert's Bar took on a new mission—patrolling the beaches and serving as lookouts from the refuge's newly constructed watchtower.

Miami Beach

1915–Present · Miami Beach

"Collins was the last main road you could take north or south—then it was either sand or ocean. . . . There used to be big mansions on the oceanfront, before the big hotels. When times changed, they sold the mansions and auctioned everything—my father came home with all kinds of findings like chandeliers and china. . . . In those days, people came down just for the winter, mostly from New York, New Jersey, and Canada. My school catered to students who came in November and were gone by March. . . . So many people stayed at the hotels along the beach. Natives wouldn't even go down there until summer, when you didn't have to wait in line at a restaurant. . . . When Jackie Gleason started televising his show from the old convention center, he brought Miami up to the big time."*

—Joanne Renuart, Miami Shores native

The combined talents of businessmen John Collins, Carl Fisher, and the Lumnus brothers transformed a mangrove island off the coast of Miami into a winter playground for the rich. The completion of a bridge from Miami to Miami Beach jumpstarted construction of houses, restaurants, and hotels on the barrier island. During the land boom of the 1920s, several millionaires put down roots on the oceanfront, boosting the image of this growing city. Miami Beach was on its way to becoming the most desirable winter destination in the country when a devastating hurricane hit in 1926. Miami Beach took the brunt of it. But soon after, Art Deco-designed hotels and apartment buildings sprung up along South Beach's main thoroughfares, creating the largest grouping of Art Deco buildings anywhere. Having survived its share of challenges and hardships, Miami Beach remains one of the top resort cities in the world.

Biltmore Hotel

1926–Present · Coral Gables

"The Biltmore holds a very special place in my heart. . . . At the age of 26, my dad was the crew chief for 20 Spaniards who came to Coral Gables to build the Biltmore. My dad's gang did almost all of the ceramic tile work in the building. It was their forté. . . . If a tile was broken, most tradespeople threw the pieces away, but my dad kept them and made designs and mosaics. That was his trademark . . . . It only took 9 to 10 months to build the hotel. There was a huge workforce. . . . Now, when I attend events there, I see my father's work. I recognize his style and patterns. . . . I have four daughters who called the Biltmore 'the castle.' And now my daughters have their own daughters who still call it 'the castle.' "

—Joe Pineda, son of Diego Rosello Pineda, tile craftsman for the Biltmore Hotel

Mediterranean architecture was Coral Gables' calling card. And the Biltmore Hotel was its showplace. Even its landmark Giralda Tower imitated Spain's Cathedral of Seville. Hastily constructed in 1926 by developer George Merrick and hotelier John McEntee Bowman during Florida's land boom, the 400-room Biltmore attracted the crème de la crème with its opulent design and poolside festivities. Galas, fashion shows, and aquatic productions played out around the statue-lined pool to the delight of guests like Ginger Rogers, Judy Garland, and Bing Crosby. Tarzan actor Johnny Weissmuller got his start as a swim instructor at the Biltmore's pool, where he later broke the 200-meter freestyle world record.

Venetian Pool

1924–Present · Coral Gables

"It's a gorgeous place, just like being in another world. . . . *I remember years ago, in between movies at the Olympia Theatre, we watched a newsreel showing a beauty pageant at the pool. Ladies walked out on the island with these long bathing suits and stockings—nothing like the bikinis of today. . . . I grew up in Miami during the Depression, so we didn't have money for swim lessons. . . . I had 10 children, and all of them took lessons at the Venetian Pool. On my 10th child, I finally joined the club and learned how to swim myself. . . . My kids still complain about how I made them get in that cold water! It comes right out of an aquifer beneath the pool. They used to drain the pool every night and refill it each day."*

—Rose Marie Morris, retired swim instructor and
member of the Venetian Aquatics Club

Transforming a limestone quarry pit into a tropical paradise was no easy feat. But in 1924, Coral Gables developer George Merrick and his talented team did just that. Showcasing Merrick's dedication to Mediterranean-style architecture, ornate towers and bridges welcomed guests into a lagoon surrounded by grottos, fountains, and waterfalls. The Venetian Pool's exotic atmosphere attracted movie stars, dignitaries, and bathing beauties, not to mention locals who danced the night away to big-name orchestras. Swimmers still flock to its cooling waters, which rise up from natural artesian wells and hold at a refreshing 76°F year-round.

Green Turtle Inn

1947–Present • Islamorada

"It was originally built for train traffic, before the road came through the Keys (the old railroad bed is today's road). Back then it was called the Rustic Inn—it was a restaurant, filling station, and bar. It made quite the business. . . . The railroad was destroyed by the hurricane, Labor Day, 1935. The Rustic Inn was one of three or four buildings remaining—those who survived met there the next morning to see who made it through the storm. . . . Sid and Roxie opened it later as the Green Turtle Inn . . . they served turtle steak and soup—it was one of the few places in the country, outside of Key West, where you could buy turtle. It brought in a lot of people . . . Hollywood types, governors, and business owners. . . . They had a cannery across the street—it shipped all over the country."

—Irving Eyster, archaeologist, author, and Keys resident since 1947

Sid and Roxie Siderious knew how to make a splash at the grand opening of their small restaurant on the Overseas Highway: offer free food and drink. The Green Turtle Inn first served up hospitality in the Keys in 1947 when residents were few and far between. Previously known as the Rustic Inn, this modest building survived the 1935 hurricane that destroyed much of Islamorada and the upper Keys. With its visible roadside location, the Green Turtle Inn beckoned local fishermen as well as travelers on their way to Key West. But what really attracted customers were its fresh turtle steaks and homemade turtle soup. Considered a delicacy, turtle meat was in demand, and the Keys had a plentiful supply. But by the early '70s, the government stepped in to protect dwindling numbers of sea turtles. Even without its namesake on the menu, the Green Turtle Inn continues its seafood tradition to this day.

Bud n' Mary's Marina

1944–Present • Islamorada

"I started out at Bud n' Mary's in '49, before there were even docks. We used to tie up our boats to a coconut tree on the beach. . . . There weren't many people down here, only five guides on the island . . . we've always had the best bunch of guides— we're all friends. . . . It takes quite a while to learn the backcountry—the tides, the types of fish. There are places on the flats called 'wheel ditches' where you have to jack up your engine to get through. We've found people lost back there. . . . I like polling around looking for fish. You're hunting them, not just putting bait out and trolling. . . . The backcountry is a beautiful place—there are flamingos eating all over the flats and thousands of white pelicans. I could go back there every day. It's all I've ever done. It's in my blood."*

—Cecil Keith, Keys native and lifelong fishing guide

Bud and Mary Stapleton set up shop in the In the Florida Keys, where the waters of the Atlantic Ocean, Florida Bay, and the Gulf Stream come together at a group of islands called Islamorada—now known to many as "the sport fishing capital of the world." In 1944, Bud N' Mary's Marina was little more than a mom-and-pop bait shop, boat rental, and local fisherman's hangout. But as the Key's fish stories grew, affluent northern anglers headed south to try their luck, and needed local guides to lead them. With help from Bud N' Mary's native captains and seasoned guides, visitors explored the backcountry and fished offshore, returning with record catches. Over the years, Bud N' Mary's Marina became the hub of the Key's fishing excursions, with its highly regarded guides at the helm.

Long Key Viaduct

1912–Present · Florida Keys

"I've talked to a lot of old timers who remember riding the train and having the feeling of being at sea. When you looked out any window, all you saw was water. It felt as though you were aboard a ship. . . . Long Key bridge was one of a kind. It was tailored and textured more than the rest of them. Each arch was framed with bas-relief embellishments. Only boaters and fishermen could enjoy it, though—passengers couldn't see the bridge from the train. . . . We aren't sure why it was built so much better. We can guess that since Long Key was where Flagler had a first-class fishing camp, maybe he was trying to create an illusion of grandeur."*

—Jerry Wilkinson, fourth-generation Floridian and president of the
Historical Preservation Society of the Upper Keys

Gracing the cover of brochures, advertisements, and postcards, Long Key Viaduct was once the trademark image of railroad magnate Henry Flagler's Overseas Railroad. Connecting Miami to Key West, this extension of the Florida East Coast Railway was a feat of engineering, logistics, and manpower. But all did not go smoothly. In 1906, a hurricane drowned 150 laborers housed in a quarter boat just as the viaduct was taking shape. The first major bridge of many along the line, Long Key Viaduct boasted over two miles of decorative cement arches stabilized in coral rock. Nearby was the exclusive Long Key Fishing Club, made famous by author and fishing enthusiast Zane Grey. When The Key West Extension came on line in 1912, it was known as "the eighth wonder of the world."

149

Patty DiRienzo

Patty DiRienzo spent more than a decade as an award-winning photojournalist for newspapers and magazines in the Southeast and Midwest, including *The Virginian Pilot* and *City Magazine*. After moving to Florida she focused her talents on hand coloring black & white portraits and creating image transfer art. Both hand-crafted techniques replicate the nostalgic look of vintage photographs. She also worked as a contract photographer for Silver Image, a photo agency specializing in Florida-related editorial assignments. Her credits include the *New York Times, USA Today,* and *Time*. In 2002, Patty received a grant from the Florida Humanities Council for her photo project, *Florida: A Journey Through its Colorful Past*. She was also selected to exhibit her work in the Heritage Gallery at the Museum of Florida History.